He Wakes Me

by Betsy James · illustrated by Helen K. Davie

ORCHARD BOOKS · NEW YORK

Orchard Books
A division of Franklin Watts, Inc.
387 Park Avenue South
New York, NY 10016

Manufactured in the United States of America
Printed by General Offset Company, Inc.
Bound by Horowitz/Rae
Book design by Alice Lee Groton

10 9 8 7 6 5 4 3 2 1

The text of this book is set in 20 point Diotima.
The illustrations are watercolors.

Library of Congress Cataloging-in-Publication Data
James, Betsy.
  He wakes me/by Betsy James; illustrated by Helen K. Davie.
     p.   cm.
Summary: A little girl describes her cat's life from his waking
her in the morning to his putting her to sleep at night.
ISBN 0-531-05954-5.—ISBN 0-531-08554-6 (lib. bdg.)
1. Cats—Juvenile literature.   [1. Cats.]   I. Davie, Helen. ill.
II. Title.   SF445.7.J34   1991   90-28920

For Zephyr, Zoot, and Backyard Boris

—B.J.

To the cats who woke us before:
John Muir, Mona, Naomi;
and the cats who wake us today:
Tyb, Kate, Gwen;
and all the cats we have yet to meet.

But especially for Frank,
the man who made room in his heart
for all my cats and me.

—H.K.D.

He wakes me with his feet.

His toes are soft,
with hidden needles.

He sits on me,
his four feet
close as a cloverleaf,
his tail
laid neatly behind.

He has been out all night,
and smells like the rain.

When I stretch,
he stretches.
His tail asks a question.

He jumps down,
and I get up.

He yells at breakfast.
He doesn't use a spoon.

He licks his paws, and uses them
to wash his face.

He has his coat on already.
He needs me
to open the door.

Where does he go,
slanting off
under the lilac bush?

He goes under.
He goes through.
He goes everywhere
that is too narrow for me.

He knows the world
the way a needle knows wool,
slipping through it.
He knows the roses.

He knows
what lives
on the underside of a leaf.

At lunchtime
his tongue is a mop.
His whiskers are a broom
for every crumb.

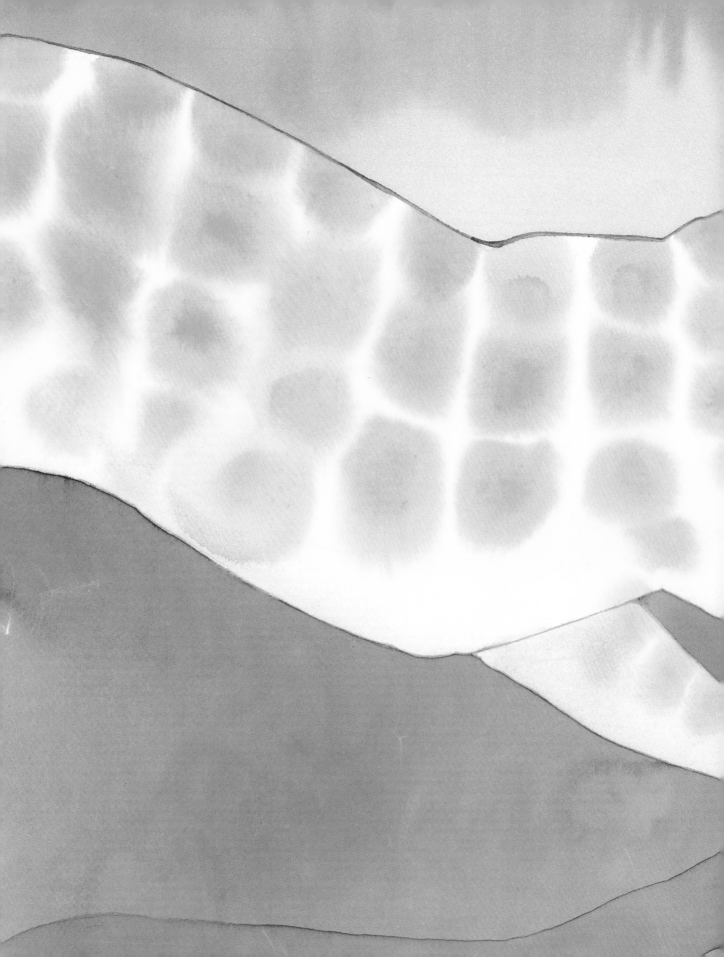

He can run whenever he wants.
Everything
with a string
is a mouse.
Everything that flutters
is a sparrow.
Everything that rustles
is a leaf.

I am taller than he is,
but he climbs higher.

I am stronger than he is,
but if he wants to leave
I can't hold him.

He hates to swing.

But he knows about naps.

He sleeps in a circle.
He curls up
behind my knees.

The sun comes looking for him.
It squares him
in all its window frames
and turns
his fur
to fire.

At supper
he sings about chicken.
He thinks liver is dessert.

At the fireplace
he tucks away
everything but his ears.
He would fit in a shoe box.

His ears are velvet leather,
with nicks.
What is softer than he is?
However I touch him,
he fits.

He has no bedtime.

He can stay up forever.

He knows
what the wind does at night.
He knows
who walks past on the sidewalk
when the moon shines down the chimney.
He knows
what the house smells like
when it is full of dreams.

His purr is sleepy as a story.
He is heavy
as a pillow.

He is warm.
His eyes are quiet.
With his feet
he pats me to sleep.